Kings Canyon: The Backpacker's Park

I0438849

Dale Matson

Acknowledgements

Sharon Matson Editing
National Geographic TOPO Maps
Carrie Help with Adobe Software

Kings Canyon: The Backpacker's Park

Preface

It may seem odd that I would begin this piece talking about Yosemite alongside Kings Canyon. With over twenty years of trail running, hiking, backpacking and nearly ten years of search and rescue in both locations, I have slowly come to the conclusion that while Yosemite may be the preferred *tourist* destination, Kings Canyon is the place for *backpackers*. This is not to say that there is not excellent backpacking in Yosemite. For example, the John Muir Trail travels through 37 miles of Yosemite with the northern terminus of the JMT in Yosemite Valley at Happy Isles.

The primary reasons for the notoriety of Yosemite and the lesser-known status of Kings Canyon is *access*. There are lots of roads providing access to many of the iconic sights in Yosemite with highway 120 bisecting the entire park. World class views are available from the windows of an automobile in Yosemite. Conversely, one can drive to only a few of the many magnificent views in Kings Canyon. There is easier access to Yosemite itself from San Francisco for international travelers.

Yosemite was designated a national park in 1890 and Kings Canyon was designated a national park in 1940. Yosemite is better known and more visited. Most of the magnificent photographs of Ansel Adams were taken in Yosemite. The name of John Muir is most associated with Yosemite. Yosemite is nearly twice the size of Kings Canyon but with close to four million visitors annually, Yosemite can be one big traffic jam in July. Even the premier day hike to Half Dome now requires a permit that was introduced to reduce trail traffic and dangerous gridlock on the cables.

So, why is this about Kings Canyon? 75 miles of the JMT is in Kings Canyon National Park. I have completed this 211-mile trail, hiking it in sections over the years. This lack of access to the inner beauty of Kings Canyon, a park like Yosemite, also formed by glaciers, has also preserved much of the pristine beauty. Kings Canyon simply has a different *feel* about it. Kings Canyon is set up for backpackers with several backcountry rangers stationed along the JMT to assist backpackers. Some of the highest peaks in the Sierras are in Kings Canyon including North Palisade at 14,249'.

If you want to see this hidden beauty, you will have to do it on foot unless you are only interested in seeing the Grant Grove of Giant Sequoias. After the JMT, the second most famous backpacking route in the Sierra Nevada's is Rae Lakes, a 46 mile Loop, that begins as a 'walk in' from Road's End in Cedar Grove.

There are other sights in Kings Canyon worth visiting by less established trails like East Lake and 60 Lake Basin. Some sights have no trails for access like Gardiner Basin. There are two great rivers in Kings Canyon, the Kings River and the San Joaquin. They have carved deep gashes in granite providing awe-inspiring views for the traveler. There are also trails with wonderful views along Bubb's Creek. The 'roads' of Kings Canyon are its trails. This photo essay is an ode to the beauty of this wild and beautiful place.

Introduction

While there are no roads through Kings Canyon National Park, there are three primary trails that provide access and act as *organizing features* for this photo essay. The primary access trail from the north and the south is the John Muir Trail (JMT). The JMT enters the park from the north on the west side of the footbridge over Piute Creek. The JMT enters the park from the south over Forester Pass. The primary access trail from the west is the Bubb's Creek trail originating at Road's End in Cedar Grove. The primary trail from the east is the Kearsarge Pass trail originating in Onion Valley near the town of Independence. There are other access trails from the east like the Bishop Pass, Taboose, Sawmill and Baxter passes. The book will be divided into these three sections.

1. <u>John Muir Trail</u> including Dragon Lake and 60 Lake Basin
2. <u>Kearsarge Pass Trail</u> to Glen Pass
3. <u>Bubb's Creek Trail</u> including East Lake and Charlotte Lake

If one considers these three main trails, the Bubb's Creek and Kearsarge Pass trails can bisect Kings Canyon from east to west and the JMT, from north to south.

John Muir Trail

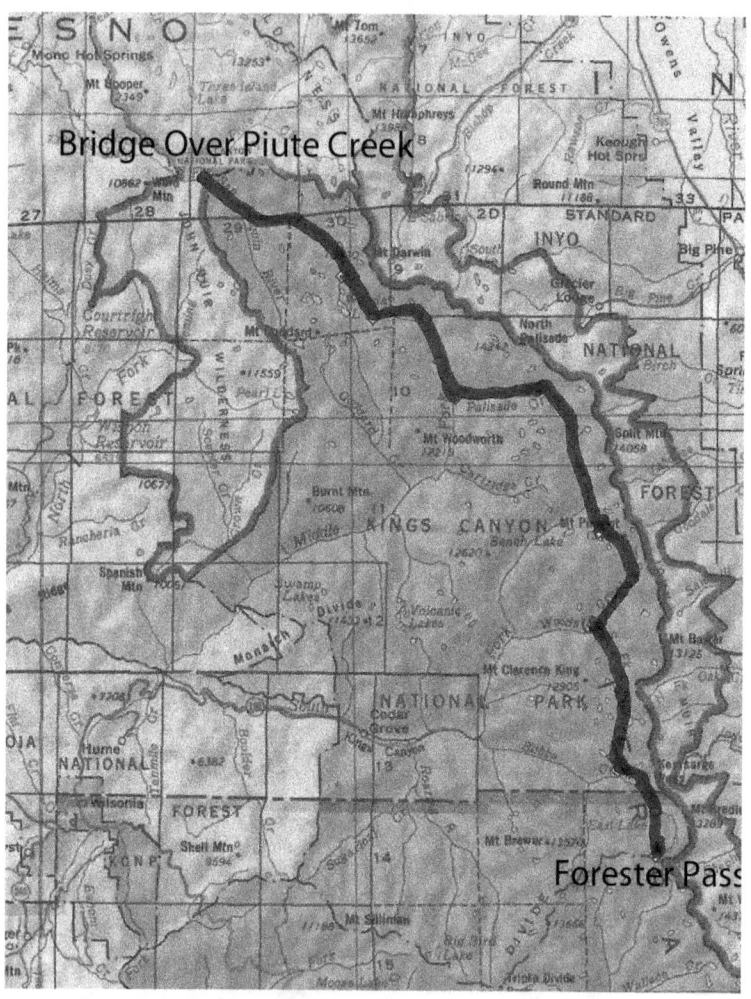

The John Muir Trail (JMT) in named in honor of the naturalist, environmentalist and explorer John Muir (1838-1914). There is a certain irony in the fact that John Muir never hiked this trail. The JMT is considered one of the finest hiking trails in the world and 75 of the 211 miles of the trail are in Kings Canyon National Park. I would add that overall, it is the most beautiful stretch of the trail that includes five of the JMT's seven major passes. Two sections were the last to be completed using high explosives to provide a trail. The first section is referred to as "The Golden Staircase" that leads up to Mather Pass (12,100') (named after the first director of the national park service) along Palisade Creek from the LeConte Canyon, which is the low point of this section of the trail at 8,000'. This section was completed in 1938 and allowed the trail to remain along the Sierra crest. LeConte Canyon was named after Joseph LeConte a U.C. Berkeley professor of geology and an early director of the Sierra Club who was also a friend of John Muir.

The other section completed later was over Forester Pass. Forester Pass is the highest pass on the 2,663-mile Pacific Crest Trail that is joined with much of the JMT. Trail Crest (13,600') on the climb to the top of Mt. Whitney is considered the highest pass on the JMT. Forester Pass was not named after a person. The pass was named after the forest service workers that constructed it. One must wonder if the JMT would even be built today or if it could pass an environmental impact study.

The Kings Canyon section of the JMT is also the least accessible with only one resupply point within miles of the trail. Access to the beginning of the Kings Canyon trail in the north is an 8-mile hike from Florence Lake. The last southbound resupply point before Kings Canyon is at Muir Camp, a short distance from where the trail enters Kings Canyon. Some folks attempt a resupply in Onion Valley with food stored in the bear boxes. Lot's of luck with that idea!

Bridge over Piute Creek

San Joaquin River

← EVOLUTION VALLEY 2.0

From Florence Lake, the Kings Canyon section of the JMT is also the least accessible with only one resupply point within miles of the trail. Access to the beginning of the Kings Canyon trail in the north is an 8-mile hike from Florence Lake. The last southbound resupply point before Kings Canyon is at Muir Camp, a short distance from where the trail enters Kings Canyon. Some folks attempt a resupply in Onion Valley with food stored in the bear boxes. Lot's of luck with that idea!

Once you cross the bridge over Piute Creek you enter Kings Canyon National Park. There is a welcoming feel and a trail with a gentle upslope that follows the San Joaquin River upstream through a gorge with steep sides on either side of the river. The trail passes through boulder fields in places. I have camped along this section before the bridge that crosses the San Joaquin. Fires are permitted at this elevation but firewood is scarce. If you were going to spend the night, I would recommend being closer to the upcoming switchbacks that climb up toward Evolution Valley. Getting an early morning start will avoid climbing in the heat of the day on this exposed cliff face with no access to water.

After this, the trail follows along Evolution Creek with its many beautiful waterfalls. Perhaps the most challenging task in this section is crossing Evolution Creek. It can be quite high, cold and fast in the spring in heavy snow years. Unbuckle your pack just in case. While there are campsites in Evolution Meadow, it is not difficult to make it to Evolution Valley (9,642') to make camp. The ranger station is close, campsites are numerous and the view is amazing. There is a curtain of mountains consisting of Mt. Mendel; Mt. Spencer, Mt. Darwin and the Hermit to the South.

Before the next big climb to Evolution Lake (10,856'), there is a confusing maze of creeks that cross the trail. If you use the logs, there will be a small campsite on the other side to mark where the trail resumes. At the top of the climb Evolution Lake comes into view.

Evolution Creek Waterfall

Crossing at Evolution Creek

Deer in Evolution Meadow

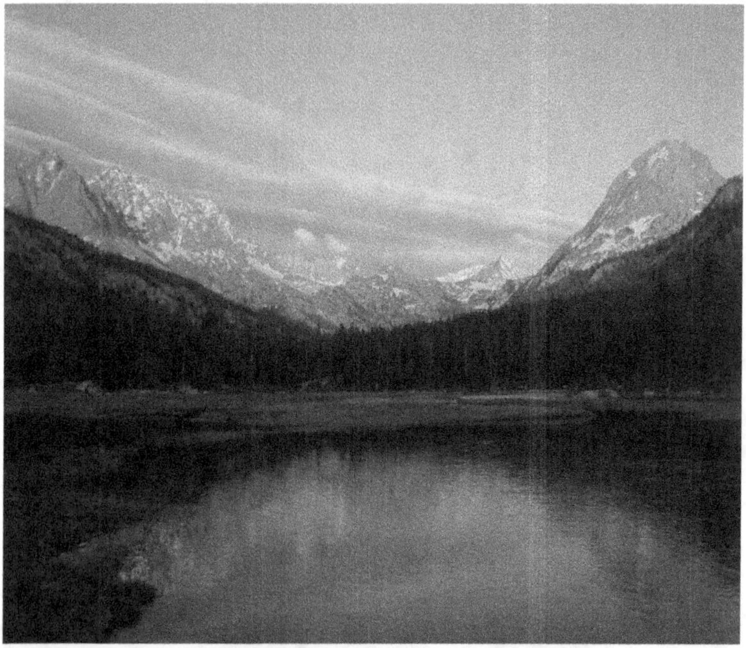

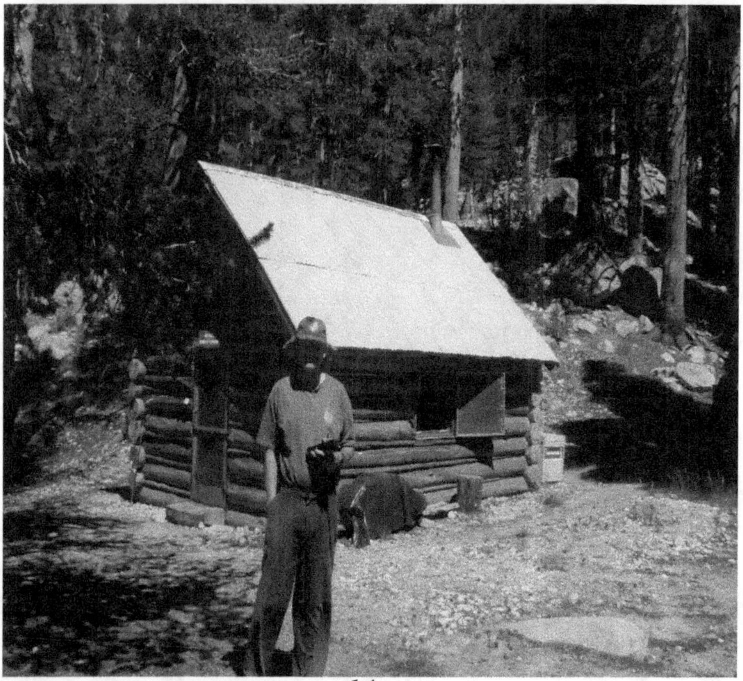

This is another popular spot for campers with most using the north shore. I camped at the northeast end of the lake below the trail. The view is breathtaking from there as well. The trail crosses a small stream at the south end of the lake and there are boulders there to help crossing.

After passing to the west of pretty Sapphire and another unnamed lake, Wanda Lake (11,430') begins to appear. Wanda Lake is named for one of John Muir's daughters. It is quite large and if you look carefully to the south-southeast you can see the Muir Hut (11,955'). If only it were as close at it looks from that location. Actually, the climb from Wanda Lake is not bad. However, the descent is difficult and seems to last forever. The trail continues to drop almost 4,000' until the Middle Fork of the Kings River and Palisade Creek intersect at about 8,000'. How sad that all of this elevation lost must be regained by the time you hit Mather Pass heading south.

The view from Muir Pass is wonderful and includes the Black Giant considerably south of the trail. The hut is intended for travelers in trouble and not usually considered for overnight stays. It was designed by the San Francisco Architect Henry Gutterson and built entirely of stone by the Sierra Club in 1930. The stones are local but the mortar and sand had to be brought in by mules. Muir Pass also divides the area to the north drained by the San Joaquin River and the south drained by the Kings River.

LeConte Canyon is deep and long with campsites in Big Pete and Little Pete Meadows. There is a ranger station (newly constructed in 2012) near the intersection of the JMT and the trail from Bishop Pass. The views are all up.

Evolution Lake at Dusk

Wanda Lake

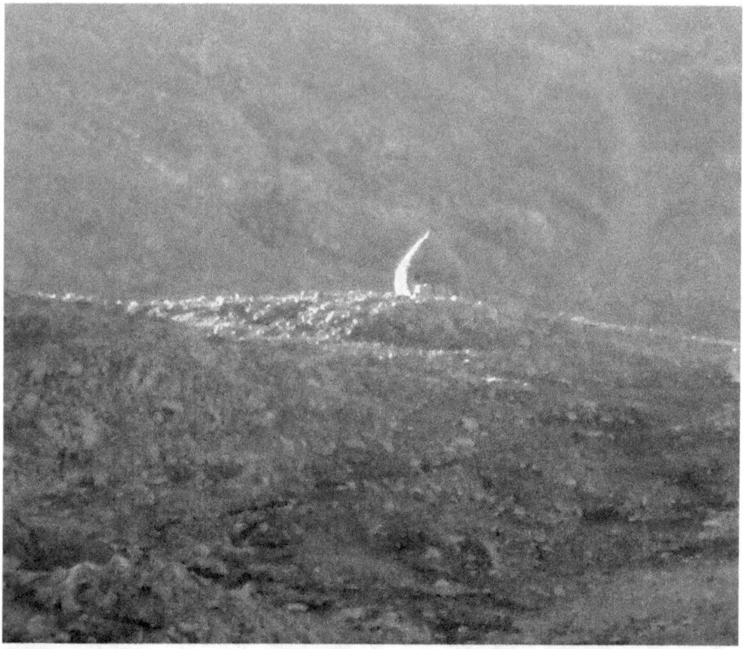

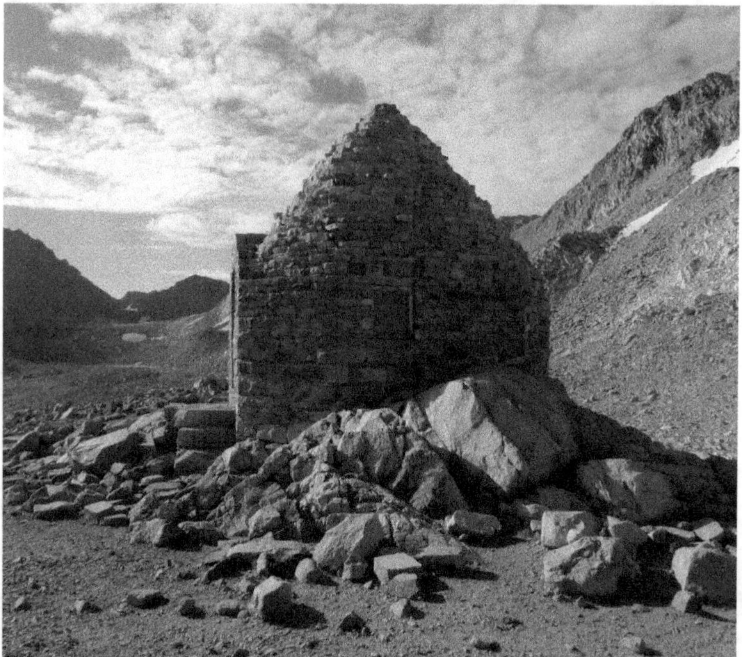

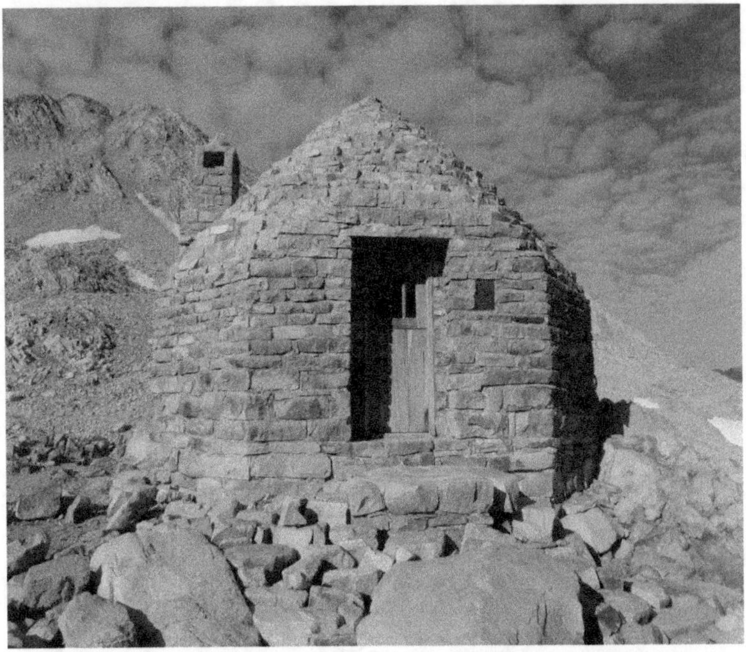

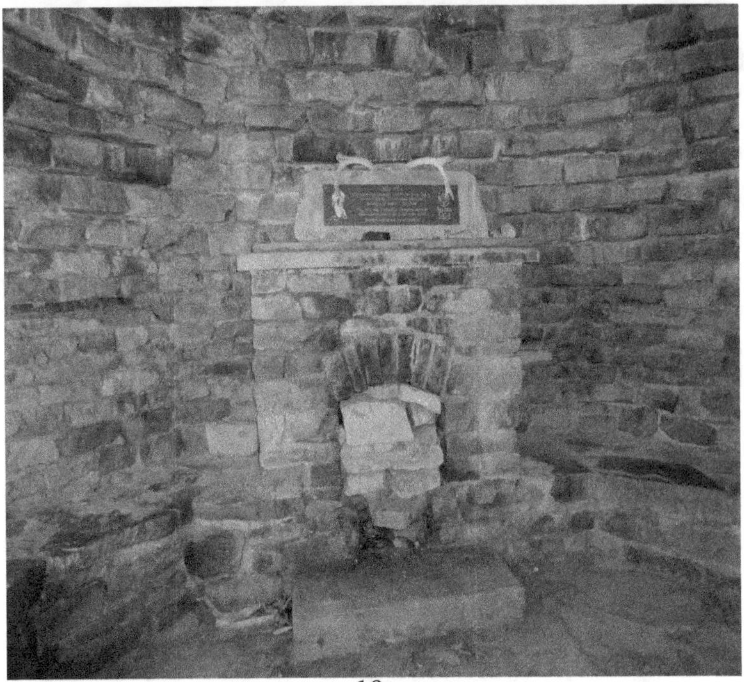

View North From Muir Pass

View South

Le conte Canyon View

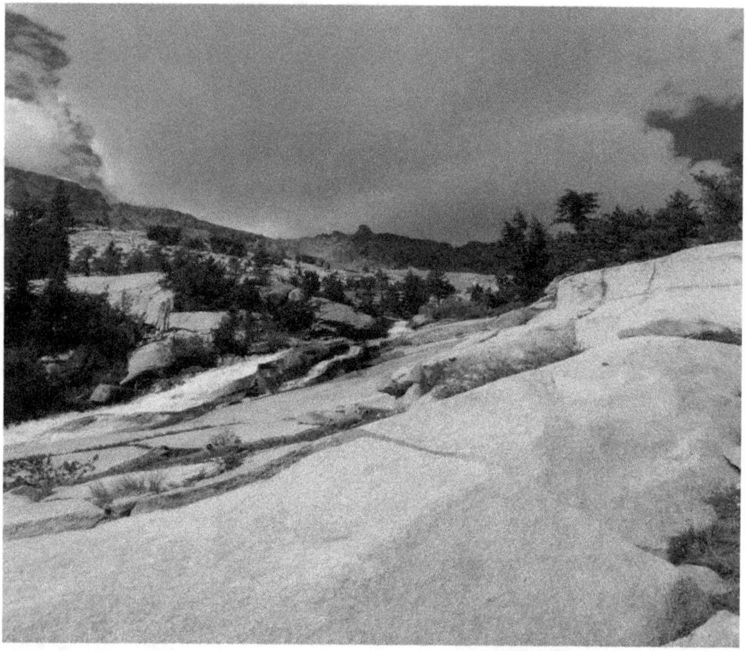

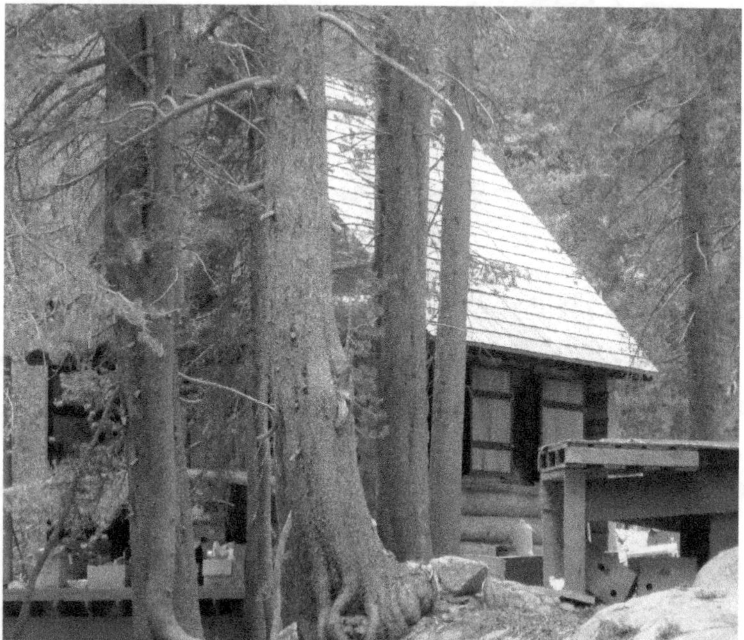

I stayed overnight in an established campsite in Deer Meadow near Cataract Creek. There was a light shower that continued into the early morning. I left at first light proceeding through an intermittent fog. Fog has a way of creating a surrealistic setting that is magnified by the mountains. As an ultra running friend Baz Halley would say, "It's magic."

Not long after crossing Glacier Creek, the trail begins to ascend in earnest. The Golden Staircase is an engineering marvel. I can't remember the downside drop of the trail because I was so immersed in the beauty of the Palisades shrouded in fog as I climbed toward lower Palisade Lake. It was a great location for downsizing the ego.

As the trail heads toward Upper Palisade Lake, it begins to climb again and is over 200' above it by the time you are beside it. The trail also curves around behind several outcroppings. I'm not sure why those who designed the trail didn't run it along closer to the second lake before ascending to Mather Pass (12,100'). The climb is fairly direct and not too difficult. The view from the pass is best looking back to the north. The descent from Mather Pass is a good trail and eventually becomes a gentle downgrade to where the trail crosses the south fork of the Kings River (10,069). The Taboose Pass trail splits as it approaches the JMT with one fork favoring the northbound and the other fork favoring the southbound JMT. This fork crosses the JMT and ends near the ranger station at Bench Lake. This was the base for Ranger Randy Morgenson who went missing in 1996. The fascinating story of the search for him is told in "The Last Season". The Taboose Pass trail to the east side is not maintained and those who use it should be good navigators. It is lightly travelled. A man went missing on this trail in 2012 and his remains were found in June of 2013.

Pallisades In The Mist Golden Staircase

Lower Palisade Lake

Upper Palisade Lake on Climb to Mather Pass

Mather Pass Looking South

Trail Along South Fork of Kings River

Marjorie Lake

This time there is not as much altitude to regain headed toward Pinchot Pass (12,086'). The pass was named after Gifford Pinchot, the first head of the U.S. Forest Service and governor of Pennsylvania. My travels took me over both Mather and Pinchot Passes in the same day. It had been raining off and on as I approached Marjorie Lake. Other pilgrims had decided to camp and wait to cross over Pinchot Pass when the weather improved. There was distant thunder in the air when I arrived at beautiful Marjorie Lake. What a great view with colorful mountains beyond it. It looked like the storm was passing so I continued.

The endangered Sierra Nevada Bighorn Sheep have been seen all along the trail from this point all the way to Glen Pass. I talked to someone traveling northbound who had seen some ewes near Pinchot Pass. The sheep are also scattered around the Rae Lakes area and east of there in the 60 lake and Gardiner Basins.

The climb up to Pinchot Pass was merciful with an excellent trail. The rain had stopped for the climb. I called my wife on the satellite phone to let her know I was planning to spend the night near Twin Lakes. As soon as I ended the call, it began to rain again and I headed down after putting on rain pants, a hooded rain shell and waterproof gloves. I was getting tired and was glad that I was heading down again on a gracious set of switchbacks.

With daylight fading it was obvious that I would not make Twin Lakes before dark. It is off the trail also. I stopped near a little unnamed lake off to the east side of the trail before Twin Lakes and made camp, in a small grove of evergreens on the west side of the trail. I needed to use my headlamp. There was no one else nearby and it seemed somewhat lonely. The next section from where I stayed soon begins following Wood's Creek.

The distance to Wood's Creek Junction is about five miles from where I stayed overnight. This junction is where the JMT continues south to Rae Lakes (6.1 miles) and the Wood's Creek Trail, following Wood's Creek (part of the Rae Lakes Loop) heads west toward Road's End (15 miles).

Continuing south to Rae Lakes, one must first cross the famous suspension bridge over Wood's Creek. It sways with only a single person crossing it and this is a requirement stated on the sign by the bridge. There are several camping spots in the vicinity with bear boxes too. I'm not sure why there are bear boxes, because carrying a bear canister is mandatory for overnight travelers in Kings Canyon Park. This is a popular bear hangout area.

As I head south toward Dollar and Arrowhead Lakes, I am reminded that, while I have been traveling in Kings Canyon Park, I have also been traveling in Fresno County, my county of residence. It is easier to access this part of Fresno County from the east side of the Sierras (Inyo County). Mt. Clarence King can be seen to the west. Deer are plentiful in the surrounding meadows.

This is an absolutely gorgeous section of the trail with campsites near the lakes along the trail. Rae Lakes is such a popular section of trail because it is part of the Rae Lakes Loop trail and the JMT. There is a two-night maximum for staying in this area. Bighorn sheep have been spotted right on the trail in this area. The new ranger cabin at Rae Lakes was finished in 2012. It was a good choice to replace the tent cabins.

There are two iconic features at Rae Lakes, Fin Dome (11,693') and Painted Lady (11,854'). The reverse side of Fin Dome can be seen from 60 Lake Basin. Rae Lakes with Painted Lady in the background is simply captivating. Stop and sign in and say, "Hi" to the ranger. Ask him if he has heard of any sheep sighting lately. Dave Gordon was the most recent ranger there.

Pinchot Pass

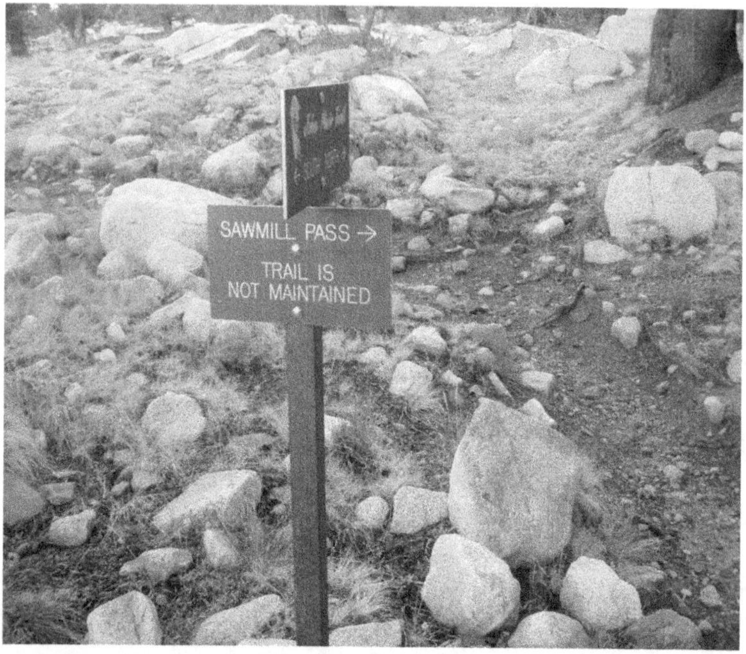
SAWMILL PASS →
TRAIL IS
NOT MAINTAINED

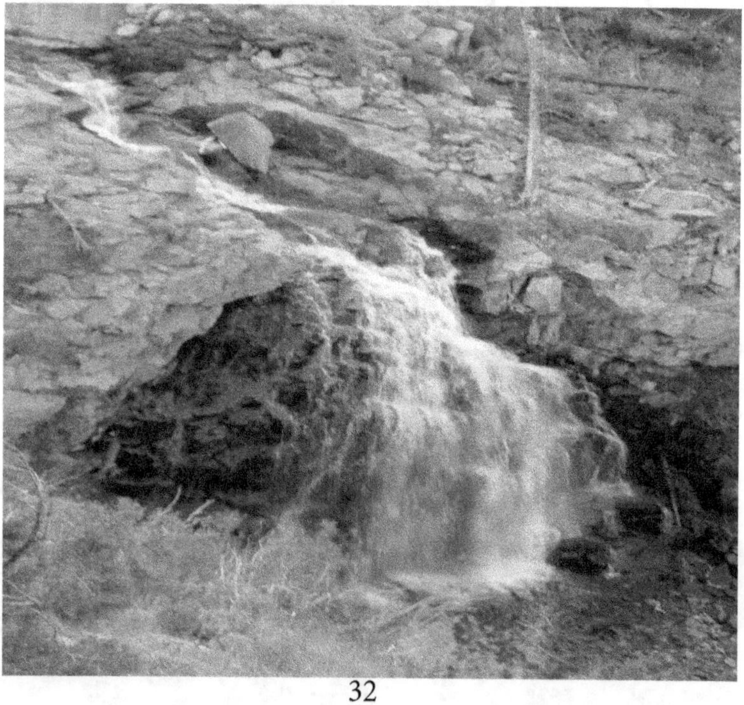

Suspension Bridge at Wood's Creek

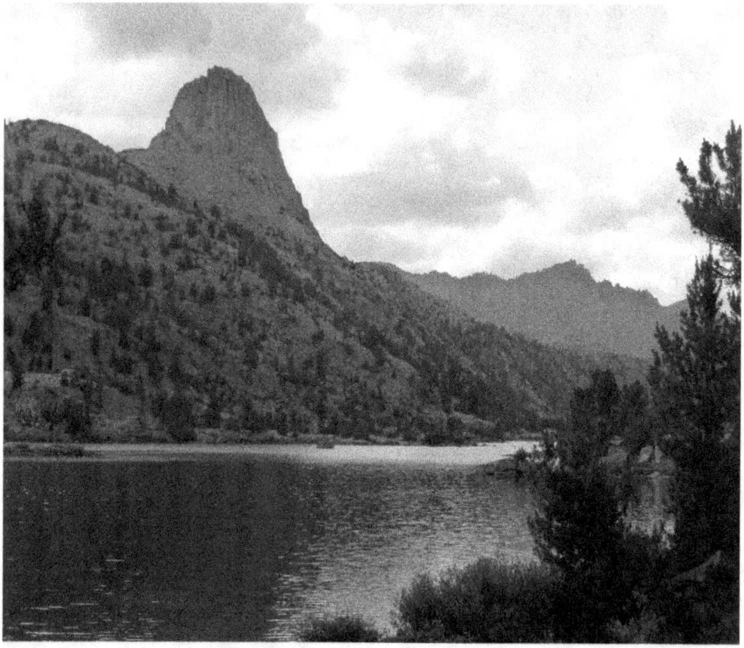

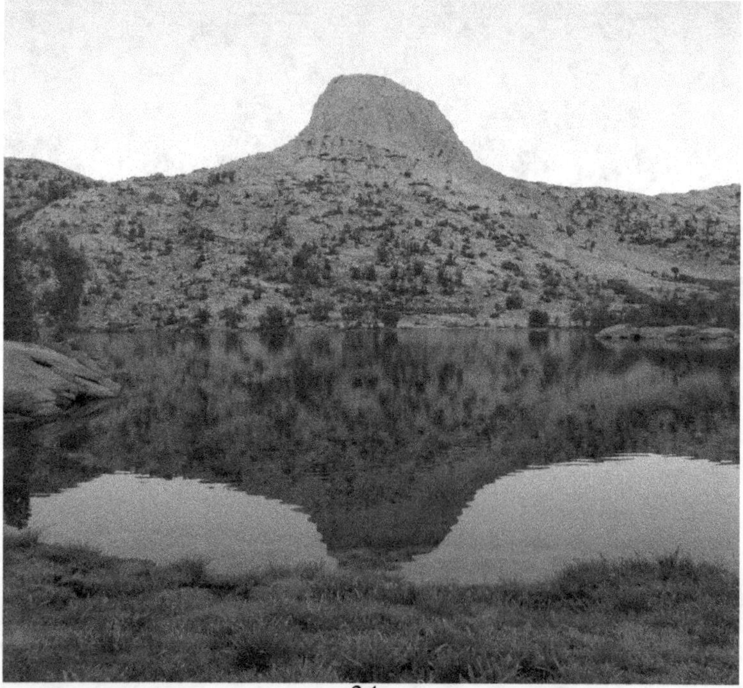

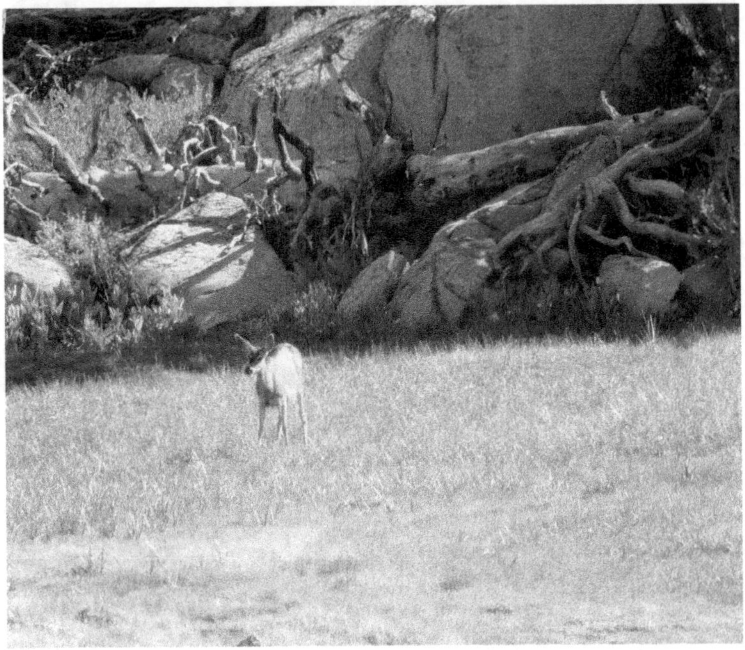

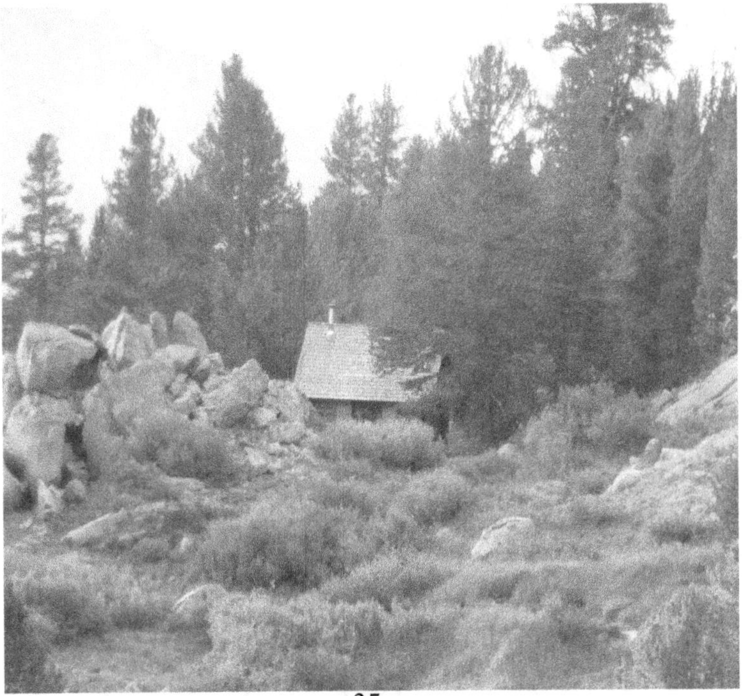

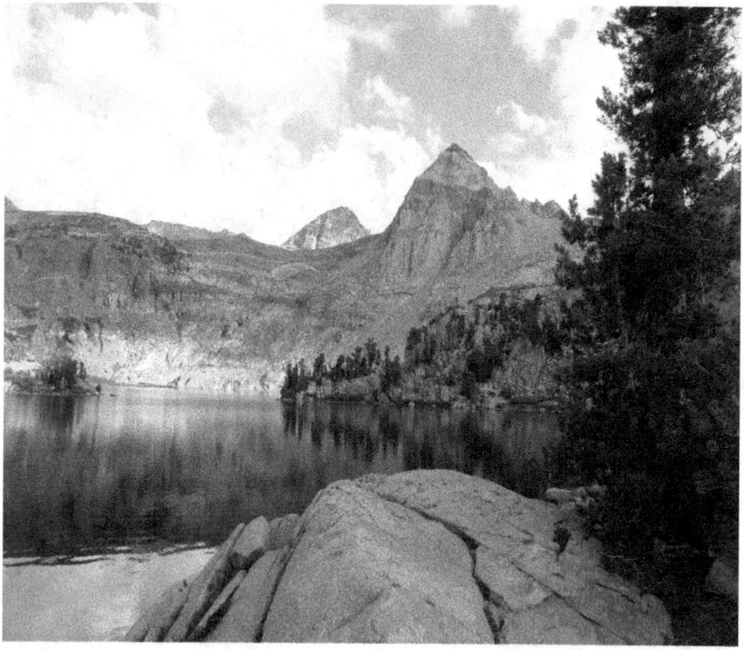

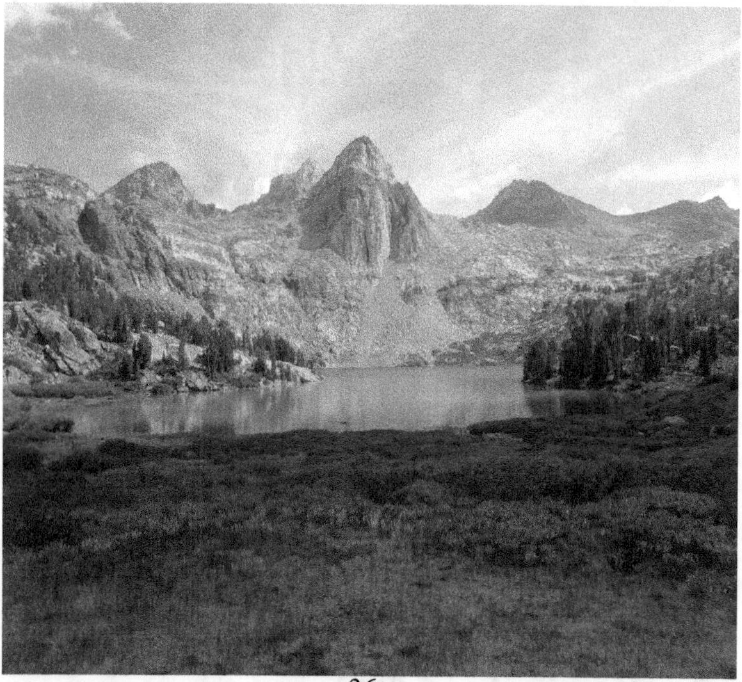

Campsite With Painted Lady In Background

Dragon Lake

As noted earlier. There are two routes worth exploring off the JMT in the Rae Lakes area. There is a use trail at the end of lake "3212" (10,545') in Rae Lakes. Dragon Lake (11,079) is nestled in a bowl and is difficult to see unless you are there. There is no sign for the trail but the trail is evident as it heads toward Dragon Lake from the JMT. It is a bit of work to go less than a mile because of the steep climb. At times, there is no trail at all. If all else fails, keep in mind that the 'route' is north of and parallels the creek route. It is truly a lovely lake isolated from the rest of Rae Lakes. There are good camping spots on either side of the creek outlet at the northwest end of the lake. Bighorn sheep hang out here although I didn't see any when I was there. The climb also provides a great view of Rae Lakes.

View Of Rae Lakes on Climb To Dragon Lake

60 Lake and Gardiner Basins

The 60 Lake Basin trail is less than half a mile south-bound from the Dragon Lake cutoff trail. There is a sign for this trail and it is established by heavier use. There are several good campsites near the beginning of the trail and I have enjoyed the view of Painted Lady from there. There is also a nice campsite/view by the first lake near the top of the climb out of Rae Lakes. After an initial flat section, it climbs up and over and back down a ridge that runs between this trail and the JMT. The two trail elevations are similar also. The trail is obvious initially but becomes less obvious as it swings north and parallels the JMT. I have not taken it to where it eventually disappears.

At the point that the trail swings north, you leave the trail and head toward what used to be called "Long Lake" (Lake 3304, 10,856'). After crossing a creek at the north end of the lake, head toward Mt. Cotter col (notch) on the ridge above. There are some hints at a trail with an occasional cairn placed. The general direction of travel is south-southwest. There are a few false summits along the way with small lakes to navigate around. The view is grand. Time limited me from going beyond a view of Gardiner Basin. We have the glaciers to thank for carving out these basins, leaving behind alpine streams and lakes (tarns). This trail is an out and back to the JMT. I saw my only two Bighorn Sheep above the 60 Lakes Basin trail near the sign that said, "No Stock Beyond This Point".

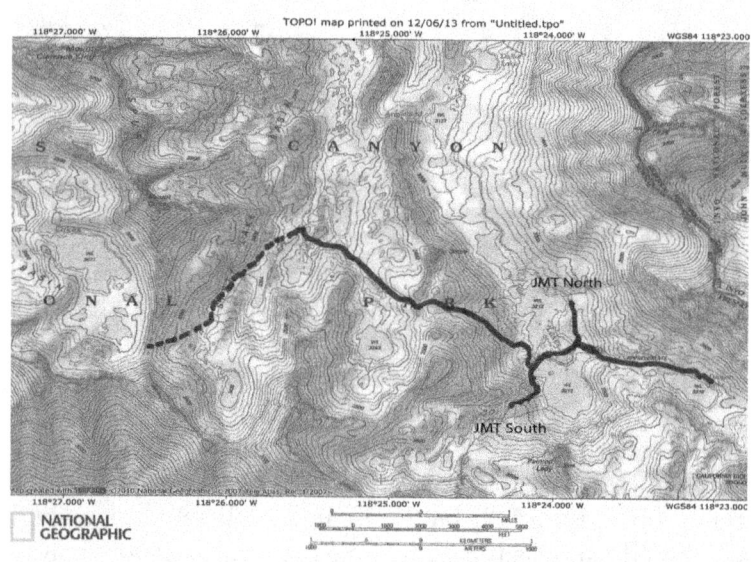

View of Rae Lakes From 60 Lake Basin Trail

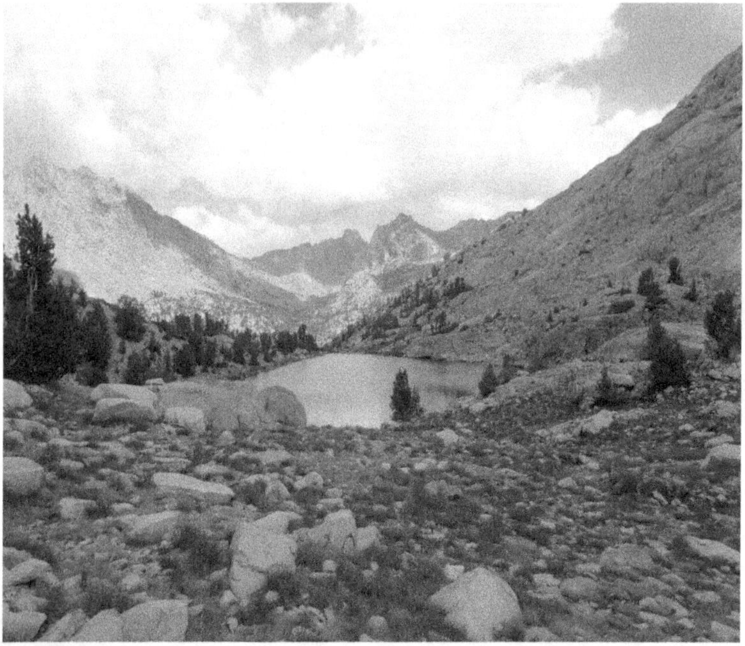

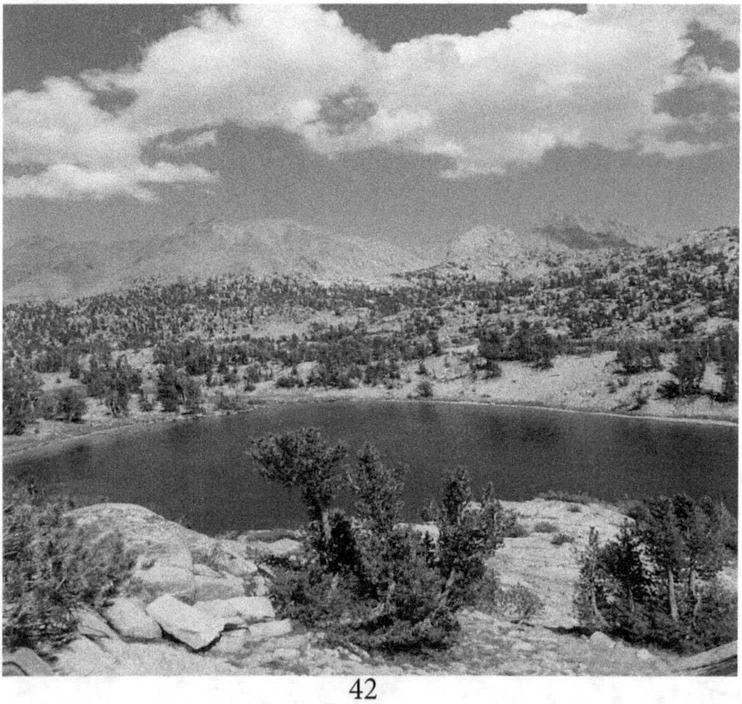

Long Lake

Mt. Cotter on Right and Gardiner Basin

The JMT Continuing South

The trail begins to climb, heading south out of Rae Lakes and doesn't stop climbing until Glen Pass. Resupply water before the switchbacks begin since there is no access to water again until halfway down the south side of the pass. Bighorn sheep have also been spotted along this section of trail including the heights surrounding Glen Pass.

I like this section of trail for the gentle descent and broad vistas that include Charlotte Dome and Charlotte Lake to the west and Vidette Peak and Bullfrog Lake to the south. Because of overuse, Bullfrog Lake has been closed to camping for years to allow it to recover.

The Kearsarge Pass trail splits east of Bullfrog Lake with one leg favoring the JMT northbound and the other favoring the JMT southbound trail. The northern section remains about 500' higher, which is not immediately evident on the topographical map. Both legs meet the JMT above Bullfrog Lake. The northern section travels through woods and the hiker must pay attention to the trail.

South of Bullfrog Lake there is access to water for resupply. There are campsites in both Vidette and Lower Vidette meadows with bear boxes also. The website climber. org has a list of all the bear boxes for the area. The Bubb's Creek trail meets the JMT at Vidette Meadow. At this point there is a sign indicating that Forester Pass is 7 miles. Bubb's Creek itself is not close to the JMT until after Lower Vidette Meadow. Vidette Meadow is just above the low point on this descent and now the trail begins to climb once again as it heads toward Forester Pass (13,200').

While there is early access to water as the JMT parallels Bubb's Creek, at about 10,500', the water become less available and dependable. The creeks that are shown on the maps dry up. I was on this section in August of a dry year and needed to camp under the final bit of scrub pines just off the trail about 11,260'. There is a dependable and nearby creek at this location. It was also a good place to begin the final ascent to Forester Pass. There is a larger established campsite below this on the west side of the trail.

I began my final assault before daylight with a head-lamp. Several folks had already passed my campsite while I was having coffee. The route is beautiful with grand vistas, Junction Peak directly in front and unnamed lakes. This is the most civilized climb to a mountain pass I experience on the JMT. Maybe I was just in better shape and acclimated to the altitude. Be careful at Forester Pass because it's a long way down if you go the wrong way. The trail makes a sharp bend. That is the southern boundary of Kings Canyon National Park with great vistas once again.

Glen Pass Looking North

Charlotte Dome

Charlotte Lake From JMT

Vidette Peak

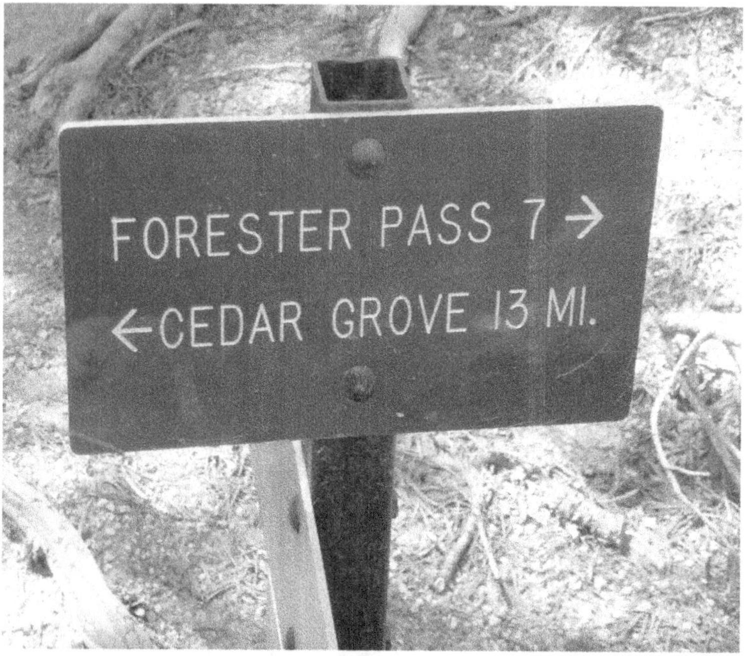
FORESTER PASS 7 →
← CEDAR GROVE 13 MI.

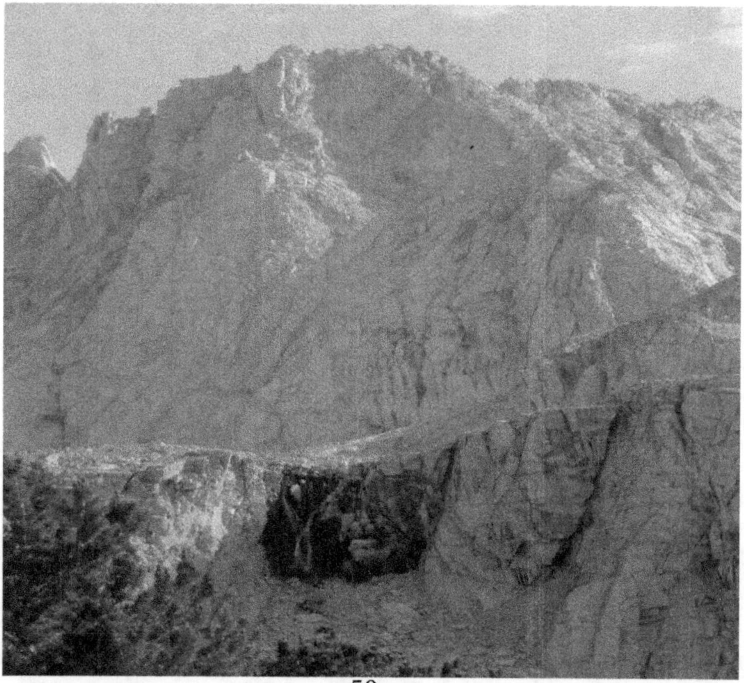

Bubbs Creek With Junction Peak In The Distance

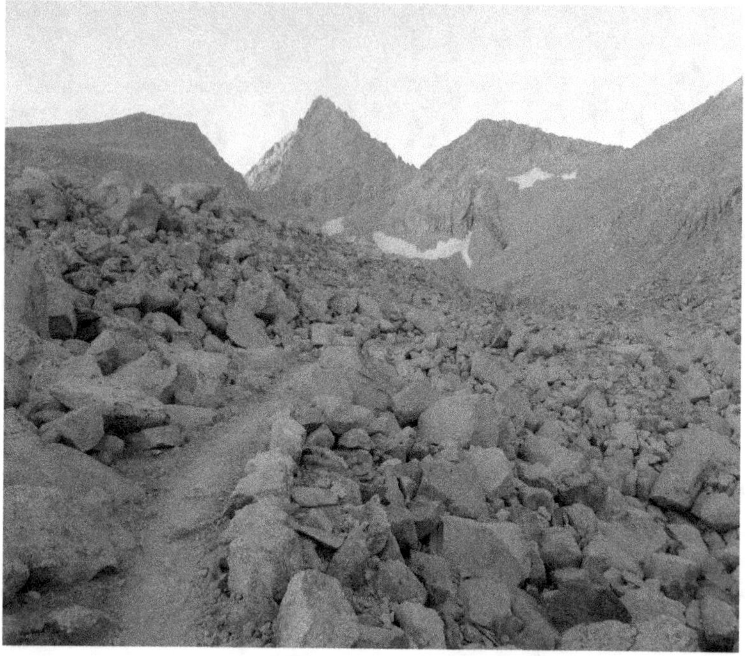

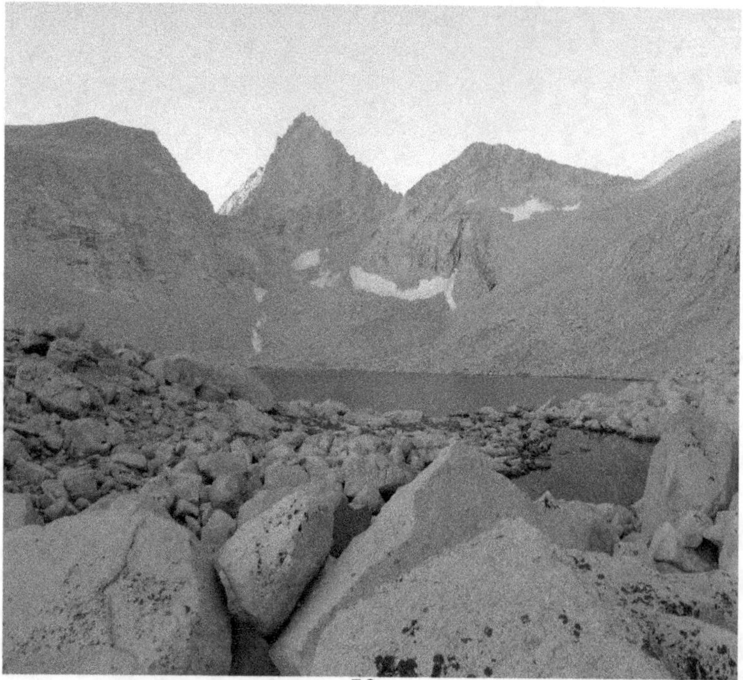

ENTERING
SEQUOIA NATIONAL PARK
FORESTER PASS
ELEVATION 13,200 FT.

View South From Forester Pass

Kearsarge Pass Trail To Glen Pass

While the border of Kings Canyon Park is at Kearsarge Pass, it is useful to initially talk about the trailhead (9,200'). The trailhead is located in Onion Valley, with the nearest town, Independence being a 15 mile drive. There is ample parking, restrooms and potable water at the trailhead. The hike in is on a busy trail with a mix of backpackers and day hikers headed to one of the lakes along the five mile trail. Some JMT folks are looking to resupply for the final time southbound, in Independence.

This can be a hot five mile ascent of about 2,500' and there are only three water sources with easy access. The trail crosses a creek below Little Pothole Lake. The trail passes close to the shore of Gilbert Lake and finally, there is a creek near the trail that heads to Flower Lake. Wherever you decide to resupply, plan on having lots of water when you reach Kearsarge Pass, especially if you are taking the northern leg of the Kearsarge Pass Trail. Once again, be on the lookout for bighorn sheep in this area too.

When you reach Kearsarge Pass, carefully take in the wonderful view. Facing west, Mt Gould is directly above on the right. Joseph LeConte named it for his friend Wilson S. Gould. Behind is the vast Owens River Valley. To the southwest are the Kearsarge Pinnacles and the Kearsarge Lakes. Glen Pass is about five miles from here.

The Kearsarge Pass trail descends as it travels west. After about half a mile the trail splits into two parallel legs. The northern leg continues above the southern leg, which dives down toward Kearsarge Lakes. This section of trail is a gradual downhill as it passes above Bullfrog Lake, there is a great view of Vidette Peak (12,539') to the south of Bullfrog Lake. The trail meets the JMT and turns northward. Near this point, the trail begins to climb again to over 11,000' before passing Charlotte Lake 600' below. If you look carefully, you can see the ranger cabin along the eastern shore near the north end of the lake. You also pass Charlotte Dome west of the trail, with its distinctive concave shape. It is popular for climbers. I passed an all female climbing team headed back toward Kearsarge Pass after their successful ascent.

I don't know why but it seems like the toughest climb for me of the JMT passes is the last 1,000' of trail to Glenn Pass. The climb seems relentless and I have to stop and rest in a few places. The view, once again, is wonderful. The view of Rae Lakes to the north is world class.

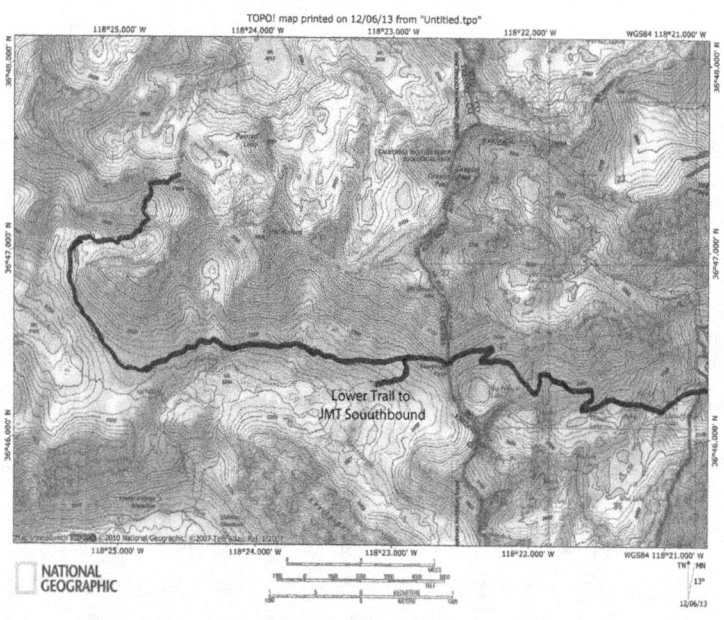

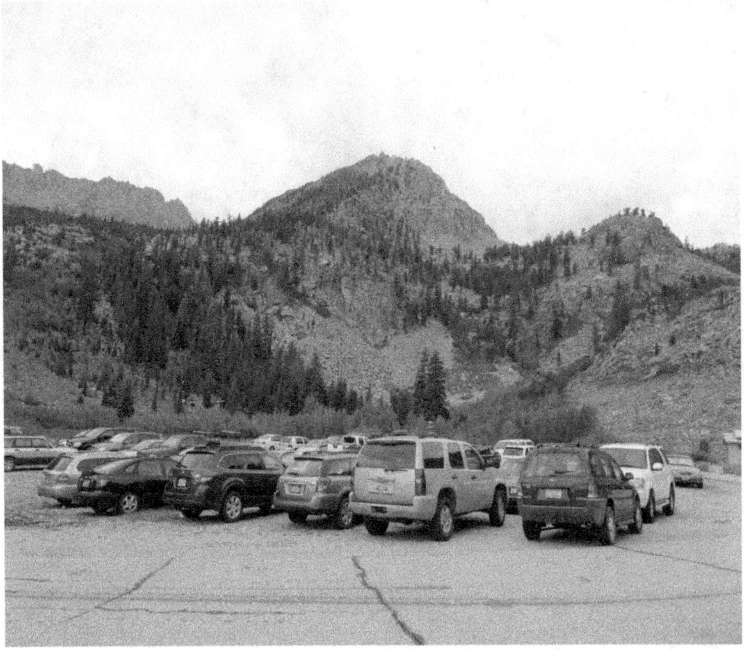

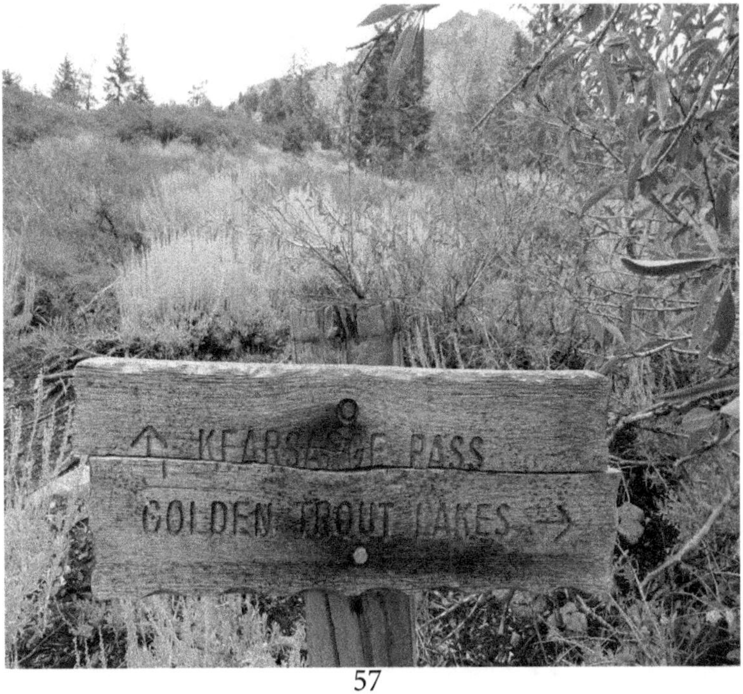
KEARSARGE PASS
GOLDEN TROUT LAKES

Big Pothole Lake

Mt. Gould From Kearsarge Pass

Kearsarge Lakes With Pinnacles Behind

Bullfrog Lake From Kearsarge Pass

60

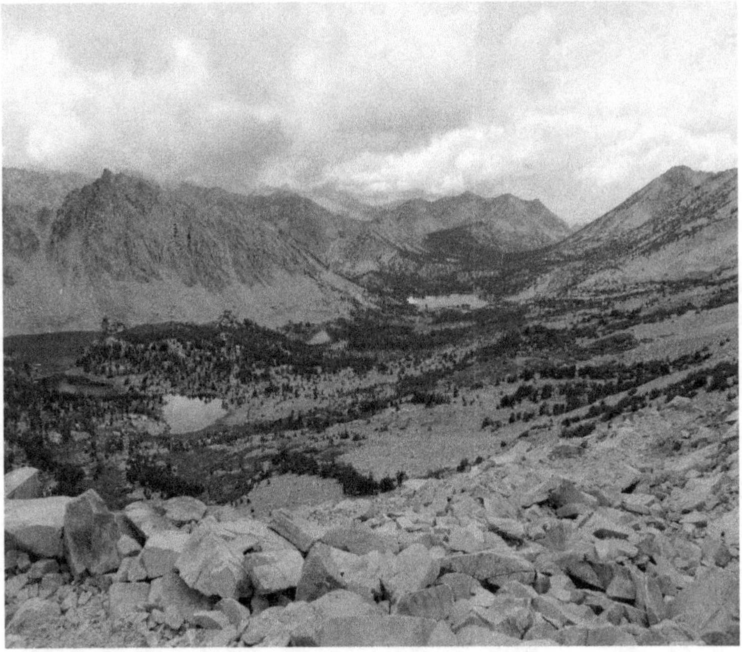

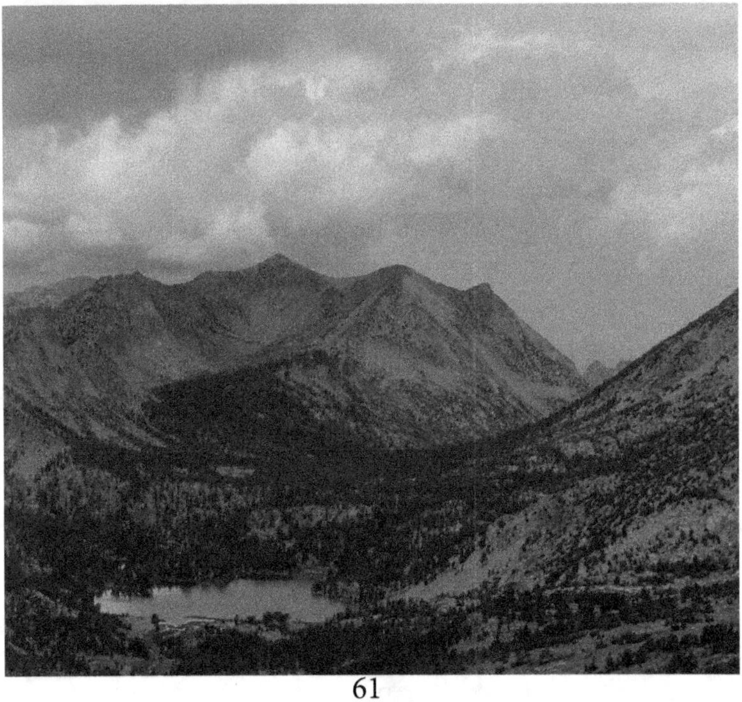

Bullfrog Lake From Kearsarge Pass Trail

KEARSARGE 0.6
LAKES
CHARLOTTE 3.0
LAKE
RAE LAKES 6.7
BULLFROG LAKE
CLOSED TO CAMPING,
GRAZING AND STOCK
TRAVEL.
KEARSARGE BASIN
CLOSED TO GRAZING
AND STOCK TRAVEL.

← CHARLOTTE 0.8
LAKE

← VIDETTE 2.4
MEADOW

RAE 4.0 →
LAKES

Little Lake On Climb To Glen Pass

View North From Glen Pass

The Bubb's Creek Trail
Including East Lake And Charlotte Lake

The trailhead for the Bubb's Creek trail is at Road's End. This is literally the end of Highway 180 in Cedar Grove. There is a wilderness permit station at the trailhead, which is the lowest point in the trail at about 5,000'. Bubb's Creek flows into the South Fork of the Kings River. Some of the other Kings Canyon trails come off from the Bubb's Creek Trail including the Sphinx Creek, Wood's Creek, East Lake and Center Basin Trails. To the east (upstream), it turns south near Lower Vidette Meadow (9,600'). It is a trail with a generally gradual climb except for switchbacks soon after the Baily Bridge at about 2.5 miles and again after Junction Meadow.

My experience with this trail is that there are not too many views, other than the Sphinx and Mt. Bago, until after Junction Meadow (12 miles). There is however, lots of wildlife including coyotes, deer, bears and even Bighorn Sheep at the higher elevations. I have seen more bears between Road's End and Junction Meadow than the rest of the park combined. Most of the time, along the trail, there is ready access to Bubb's Creek for water.

At Lower Vidette Meadow, the Bubb's Creek trail merges with the north and southbound JMT. The creek continues south (upstream) toward Forester Pass with the headwaters above tree line at about 11,300'. I have already covered the 7 miles of trail south of Lower Vidette Meadow to Forester Pass in the JMT section.

This section travels the Bubb's Creek trail to the junction with the JMT and follows the JMT north to the cutoff trail down to Charlotte Lake. I did this trip as an overnighter at Charlotte Lake and back to Road's End this summer (2013).

At Junction Meadow, I also turned south, cross Bubb's Creek and headed to East Lake (9,472'). I did this hike in 2012 as a day hike from Road's End. It is about 27 miles round trip.

The one-way trip to Charlotte Lake from Road's End is about 18 miles. The Bubb's Creek section is about 14 miles. The Junction Meadow sign distances are questionable based on my GPS distances. It is probably less than 12 miles to Junction Meadow from Road's End but it is definitely 18 miles from Road's End to Charlotte Lake!

East Lake

In Junction Meadow the 3 mile trail to East Lake (9,472) heads almost due south. It is worth the trip and there are bear boxes on both the north and south lake outlets. I have not stayed the night there. I did East Lake as a 27 mile round trip day hike from Road's End in 2012.

Let me be clear that the biggest obstacle to getting to East Lake is crossing Bubb's Creek. I forded it in late August after a low snow year. I made two previous trips and decided on both occasions against crossing because the creek was flowing so fast and deep.

After crossing the creek, the trail is somewhat sketchy but eventually becomes easier to follow. As you ascend, the views begin to open up. While some maps don't show it, there is a footbridge where the trail crosses East

Creek, going from the west side to the east side of the creek. Access to water for resupply along this trail is excellent.

When you arrive at the sign for East Lake, you are there. The trail continues beyond the sign to Reflection Lake but just head downhill toward East Lake. I had seen this lake with Mt. Brewer in the background in photographs and just had to get there. It is as beautiful as the photographs. Some folks go on to climb Mt. Brewer too, but not me.

Charlotte Lake

The strenuous climb from Junction Meadow (8,195') to Lower Vidette Meadow (9,534') is exposed and water is not always easily accessible even though the trail follows Bubb's Creek. Views begin to open up to the south as you climb. There are a couple of nice waterfalls along the way. Here you begin following the JMT north. There is another 1,000' climb from Lower Vidette Meadow to the junction with the lower leg of the Kearsarge Pass Trail coming from the east. After this the climb is less steep to the junction with the cutoff trail to Charlotte Lake that comes into the JMT from the west. There are signs at this junction as the trail to Charlotte Lake (10,387') descends about 350'. The bear boxes are near the ranger station.

TOPO! map printed on 12/06/13 from "Untitled.tpo"
118°37.000' W
118°35.000' W
118°33.000' W
118°31.000' W
118°29.000' W
118°27.000' W
118°25.000' W
WGS84 118°22.000' W
36°49.000' N
36°47.000' N
36°45.000' N
36°43.000' N
NATIONAL GEOGRAPHIC
0.0 0.5 1.0 1.5 2.0 2.5 3.0 miles
0 1 2 3 4 5 km
TN MN
13°
12/06/13

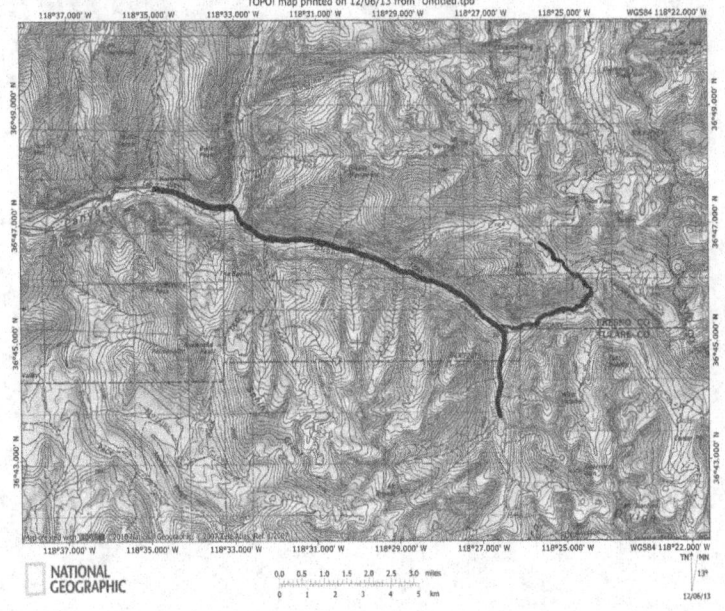

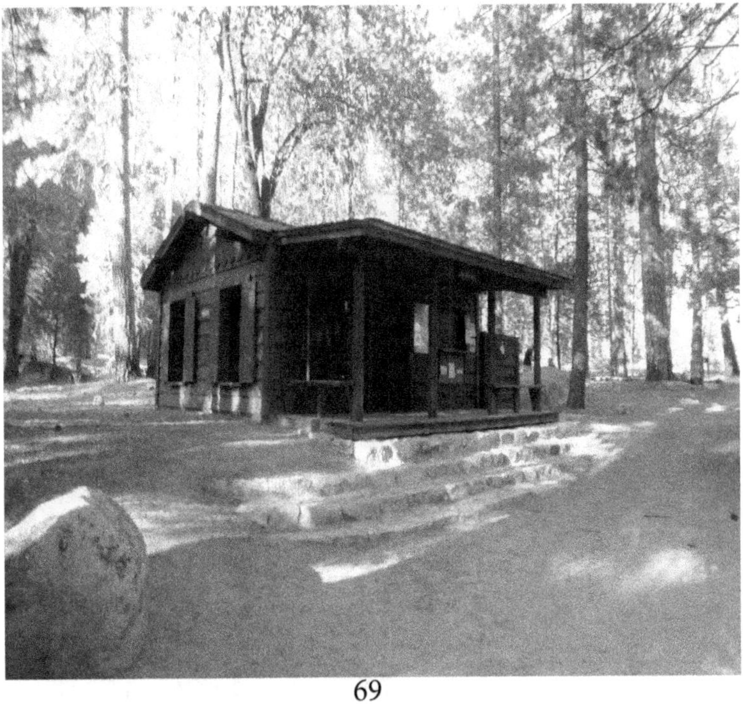

← MIST FALLS   2.7

← LOWER   4.5
  PARADISE VALLEY

← JOHN MUIR TRAIL   13.5

  SPHINX CREEK
  TRAIL JUNCTION   2.2 →

  JUNCTION
  MEADOW   8.6 →

Small Bear In Center

Sphinx

71

Bubb's Creek

JUNCTION MEADOW
← VIDETTE MDW. 2.5 MI.
ROADS END 12.0 MI. →

EAST LAKE 3.0 MI. →
LAKE REFLECTION 5.0 MI. →

Mt Bago

Crossing Bubb's Creek

East Creek

EAST LAKE

GRAZING IS NOT PERMITTED
AROUND THE SHORE OF THE LAKE.

HOLD STOCK ABOVE THE DRIFT
FENCE ¼ MILE UPSTREAM
FROM THE LAKE.

HOLDING STOCK AT YOUR
CAMPSITE IS NOT PERMITTED.

East Lake

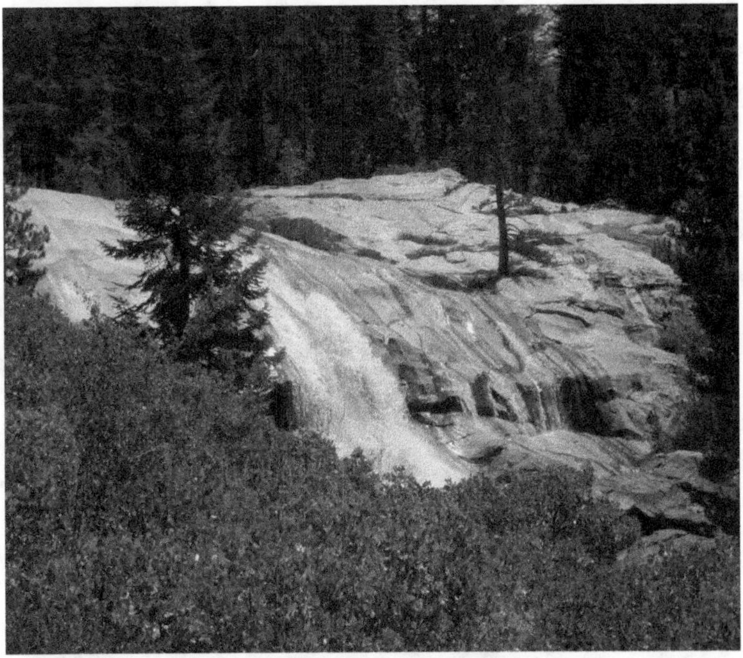

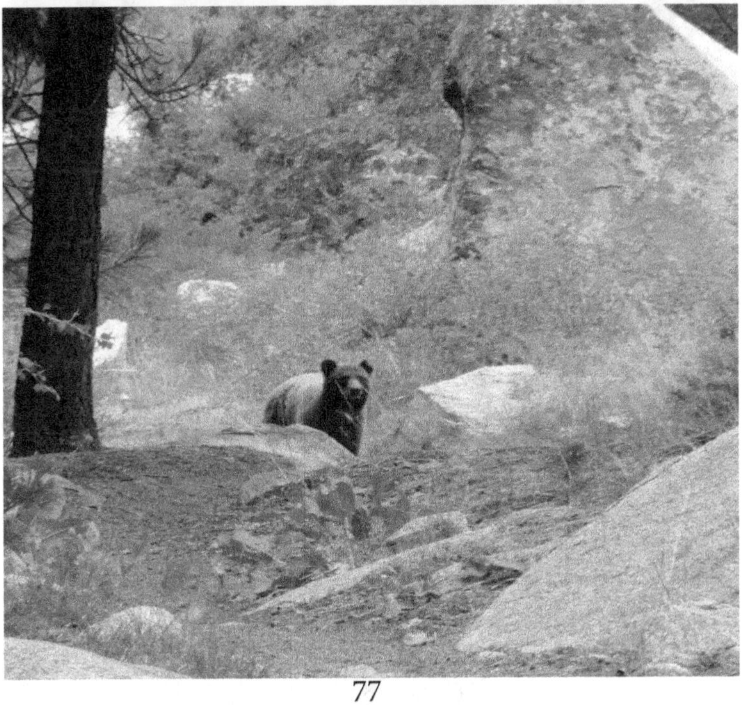

KEARSARGE PASS	3.0 →
ONION VALLEY	7.5 →
← CHARLOTTE LAKE	0.7

Trail Along Charlotte Lake

Ranger Rick Sanger

Rattlesnake

Mountains

"Great is the LORD, and highly to be praised,
And His greatness is unsearchable.
One generation shall praise Your works to another,
And shall declare Your mighty acts.
On the glorious splendor of Your majesty
And on Your wonderful works, I will meditate.
Men shall speak of the power of Your awesome acts,
And I will tell of Your greatness.
They shall eagerly utter the memory of Your abundant goodness
And will shout joyfully of Your righteousness." (Psalm 145: 3-7)

Mountains are frequently associated with God in the Holy Scriptures. Often it is a pivotal time in the history of God's people. Noah's Ark came to rest on *Mount Ararat*. Abraham took his son Isaac to *Mount Moriah* intending to sacrifice him. *Mt Moriah* is also the site of Solomon's Temple. *Mt Sinai* (Horeb) was where God revealed Himself to Moses and where the Ten Commandments were given. It was *Mount Nebo* where Moses struck the rock to provide water. It was *Mount Zion* where David built his palace and it was the *Mount of Olives* where Jesus delivered His sermon and where He was arrested. *Mount Tabor* is traditionally understood to be the place of His transfiguration. Even one of God's names, El Shaddai can be translated "God of the Mountain" (NJB).

I was born and raised in Michigan where my family also visited the Porcupine Mountains near Lake Superior in the Upper Peninsula. As a child they seemed imposing at about 1,600' of elevation. In the mid 1960's a friend of mine Dan McCosh and I drove to California from Michigan in June and I saw mountains, real mountains, for the first time. As we approached Loveland Colorado, The Rockies emerged immediately and abruptly from the plains. My heart nearly stopped as we anticipated driving over Loveland Pass at nearly 12,000', my hands immediately began to sweat. There was still considerable snow along the sides of the road as we crossed the Continental Divide. This view of the Rocky Mountains approaching Loveland made such an indelible impression on me that I knew someday I would live in an area where I could view and travel in God's glorious mountains.

Now, in my twentieth year in Fresno CA, when the air is clear I can see much of the central Sierra Nevada Mountains. The mountains offer year round recreation and I am there once a week. There is no way to describe how my spirit is elevated each time I drive east into the mountains to begin a new adventure with friends or in the company of my Airedales Susie and Duke who change from pets to companions who especially enjoy the winter snow. I also spent four of the best days of my life with my sons as we backpacked a portion of the John Muir Trail together. Hearing them talking together as men around a campfire as I fell asleep in my tent was as beautiful a sound as any waterfall or river.

These mountain places are where I fellowship with God too for it was He who made these things and us also. It can at times be as intimate an occasion for me as when I proclaim the words of the Great Thanksgiving during the Holy Eucharist.

Climb the mountains and get their good tidings. Nature's peace will flow into you as sunshine flows into trees. The winds will blow their own freshness into you, and the storms their energy, while cares will drop off like autumn leaves. ~John Muir